FIRST SOURCE TO

VOLLEYBALL

RULES, EQUIPMENT, AND KEY PLAYING TIPS

by Tyler Omoth

Consultant: William Tatge
Head Women's Volleyball Coach
Assistant Men's Volleyball Coach
Lees-McRae College
Banner Elk, North Carolina

CAPSTONE PRESS
a capstone imprint

W9-BEG-063
SOURCE

First Facts are published by Capstone Press,
1710 Roe Crest Drive, North Mankato, Minnesota 56003
www.mycapstone.com

Copyright © 2018 by Capstone Press, a Capstone imprint. All rights reserved. No part of this publication may be reproduced in whole or in part, or stored in a retrieval system, or transmitted in any form or by any means, electronic, mechanical, photocopying, recording, or otherwise, without written permission of the publisher.

Library of Congress Cataloging-in-Publication Data
Cataloging-in-publication information is on file with the Library of Congress
Names: Omoth, Tyler, author. Title: First Source to Volleyball : Rules, Equipment, and Key Playing Tips / By Tyler Omoth.
Description: North Mankato, Minnesota : An imprint of Capstone Press, 2018. | Series: First Facts. First Sports Source | Includes bibliographical references and index. | Audience: Age 7-9. | Audience: K to Grade 3.
Identifiers: LCCN 2016059568| ISBN 9781515787839 (library binding : alk. paper) | ISBN 9781515787853 (pbk. : alk. paper) | ISBN 9781515787914 (ebook pdf : alk. paper)
Subjects: LCSH: Volleyball—Juvenile literature.
Classification: LCC GV1015.34 O56 2018 | DDC 796.325—dc23
LC record available at https://lccn.loc.gov/2016059568

Editorial Credits
Gena Chester, editor; Sarah Bennett and Katy LaVigne, designers; Eric Gohl, media researcher; Kathy McColley, production specialist

Photo Credits
Getty Images: Portland Press Herald, 11; iStockphoto: FatCamera, 21 (left); Newscom: Cal Sport Media/Erik Williams, 13, Icon SMI/Samuel Lewis, 17, ZUMA Press/Allen Eyestone, 20 (left), ZUMA Press/Jon-Michael Sullivan, 21 (right), ZUMA Press/St Petersburg Times, 7; Shutterstock: A_Lesik, 1 (background, middle), Aspen Photo, 5, Daimond Shutter, cover (background), 1 (background, top left), Dean Harty, 1 (background, top right), Jan Kranendonk, 9 (bottom), MediaPictures.pl, 19, Mitrofanov Alexander, 1, muzsy, 20 (right), Paolo Bona, cover, 9 (top), Valeria Cantone, 15

Design Elements: Shutterstock

Printed and bound in China.
004610

TABLE OF CONTENTS

INTRODUCTION

Time to Attack!

Professional volleyball players work together to set up the perfect shot. Get ready to jump and **attack** the ball like Olympic volleyball star Kim Hill. If you enjoy action and teamwork, volleyball could be the sport for you.

ORIGINS OF VOLLEYBALL

In 1895 William G. Morgan wanted a sport for young businessmen in Holyoke, Massachusetts. He wanted something that would not have as much physical contact as basketball. He used a tennis net and raised it just above the players' heads.

FACT
The International Volleyball Hall of Fame is located in Holyoke, Massachusetts, where the game was invented.

attack—to jump and hit the volleyball over the net in a downward motion

CHAPTER 1

Ready to Play!

Equipment

Volleyball is a sport that doesn't need a lot of equipment. The net, a ball, and proper shoes are the most basic pieces. Volleyball players jump a lot during a play, so they need good shoes with lots of padding. They also dive to the ground to hit the ball. Some players wear knee pads for protection.

FACT
A volleyball player may jump as many as 100 times during a match.

"Coaches and players should keep a sense of humor. The bottom line is for the coach and the team to have fun and enjoy the sport."

–*Walt Ker, assistant coach University of California, Los Angeles*

The Volleyball Court

A standard volleyball court is a large rectangle. Across the middle is the volleyball net. The top of the net is 7.33 feet (2.23 meters) high for women's competitions and 7.97 feet (2.43 m) high for men's. Each side of the court has an **attack line**. The outside edges of the court are marked by **boundary lines**. Behind the back boundary line is the **service area**.

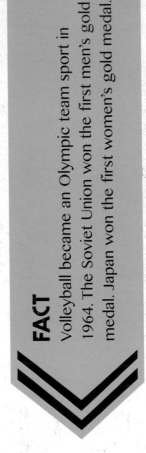

FACT

Volleyball became an Olympic team sport in 1964. The Soviet Union won the first men's gold medal. Japan won the first women's gold medal.

attack line—the line that divides the back row players from the front row players

boundary line—a line that marks the outside edge of the court

service area—the place where the server stands when putting the ball into play

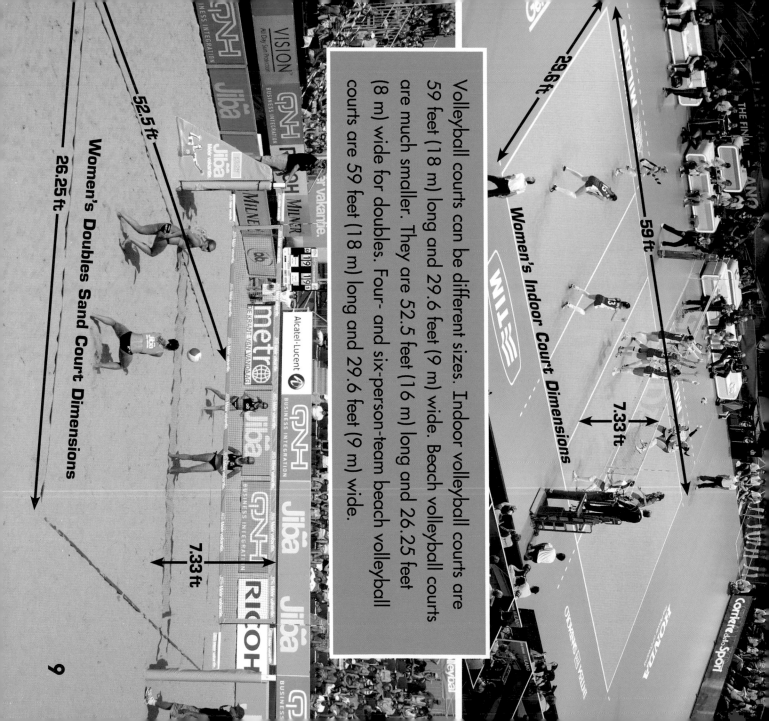

Volleyball courts can be different sizes. Indoor volleyball courts are 59 feet (18 m) long and 29.6 feet (9 m) wide. Beach volleyball courts are much smaller. They are 52.5 feet (16 m) long and 26.25 feet (8 m) wide for doubles. Four- and six-person-team beach volleyball courts are 59 feet (18 m) long and 29.6 feet (9 m) wide.

Women's Indoor Court Dimensions

29.6 ft

59 ft

7.33 ft

Women's Doubles Sand Court Dimensions

52.5 ft

26.25 ft

7.33 ft

The Positions

A volleyball team has six players on the court at a time. Hitters are best at attacking the ball and hitting it over the net. Setters pass the ball to the hitters. Middle blockers work to **block** the other team's shots. They also need to be good attackers. A libero player may enter and leave the back row as often as needed.

FACT

The United States, Brazil, and the former Soviet Union are tied for the most Olympic Gold medals in men's indoor volleyball with three each.

block—an attempt by a front row player to stop a spiked ball as it crosses the net

Setter

Hitter

Middle Blocker

Libero

CHAPTER 2

How the Game Works

Serving

Serving is a very important part of volleyball. The serve starts play. The server may choose an **overhand serve** or an **underhand serve**. Underhand serves are easier to do. They are also easier for the defense to receive. Overhand serves are difficult, but a good one could get your team an **ace**. If the ball touches the ground on the other side, your team scores a point!

overhand serve—serving the ball by striking it above the head using a fast, throwing motion

underhand serve—serving the ball by striking it with an underhand swing, using the heel of the hand

ace—a serve that hits the ground on the other team's side, giving your team a point

Types of Hits

There are several ways to hit a volleyball.

A **forearm pass** uses both arms. The player has clasped hands and holds them near the waist. The ball bounces off the player's arms below the elbows. A **set** is used when the ball is coming down above a player's head. A player uses their fingers to push the ball to a teammate. When the other team tries to hit the ball back over the net, a player may block it at the net.

forearm pass—a pass made by using the forearms

set—a pass directed to another teammate who will attack the ball

14

CHAPTER 3

Rules of the Game

Offense

The team with the ball is on offense.

The offense tries to hit the ball so that

the other team can't return it over the

net. Setters pass the ball high so a

hitter can attack it. The hitter tries to

hit the ball to part of the court where

the other team's players can't reach it.

The team that wins 3 out of 5 sets of a volleyball
match wins. The first four sets play to 25 points.
If a match goes to the fifth set, it only plays to 15.

Defense

The defense tries to keep the ball off the ground on their side. Each team can only hit the ball three times each time it comes to their side. A block does not count as a hit. Players in the front row try to block the ball. Players in the back row try to pass the ball with a forearm pass.

FACT

In the 1920s volleyball became popular on the beach. Olympic beach volleyball teams have two players and slightly different rules. It became an official Olympic sport in 1996.

CHAPTER 4

Playing Tips

Now that you know the basics, it's time to start practicing. Here are some tips to get you started.

SERVING

Create a routine when serving. Bounce the ball, take a deep breath, toss the ball, and strike! A set routine can make it easier to be consistent.

PASSING

Clasp your hands together, and turn your forearms up. You want to make a nice, flat surface for the ball to hit. Don't hit the ball with your hands. Let it hit your forearms.

SETTING

Try to get under the ball before it comes down. That way, you can hit the ball back up and to where you want it to go.

ATTACKING

The key to attacking the ball is timing. Practice jumping as a teammate sets the ball to you. You want to hit it just as you get above the net.

FACT

Bulgarian volleyball player Matey Kaziyski could hit a ball really hard. A ball he served was recorded going 82 miles (132 kilometers) per hour.

Glossary

ace (AYS)—a serve that hits the ground on the other team's side, giving your team a point

attack (uh-TAK)—to jump and hit the volleyball over the net in a downward motion

attack line (uh-TAK LINE)—the line that divides the back row players from the front row players

block (BLOK)—an attempt by a front row player to stop a spiked ball as it crosses the net

boundary line (BOUN-dur-ee LINE)—a line that marks the outside edge of the court

forearm pass (FOR-ahrm PASS)—a pass made by using the forearms

match (MACH)—a set of up to five volleyball games; to win a match, a team must win three games

overhand serve (oh-vur-HAND surv)—serving the ball by striking it above the head using a fast, throwing motion

service area (SUR-viss AIR-ee-uh)—the place where the server stands when putting the ball into play

set (SET)—a pass directed to another teammate who will attack the ball

underhand serve (UHN-dur-hand surv)—serving the ball by striking it with an underhand swing, using the heel of the hand

Read More

Bodden, Valerie. *Volleyball. Making the Play.* San Francisco, Calif: Creative Paperbacks, 2016.

Doeden, Matt. *Volleyball.* Summer Olympic Sports. Mankato, Minn. Amicus Ink, 2016.

Schwartz, Heather E. *Top Volleyball Tips.* Top Sports Tips. North Mankato, Minn.: Capstone Press, 2017.

Internet Sites

FactHound offers a safe, fun way to find Internet sites related to this book. All of the sites on FactHound have been researched by our staff.

Here's all you do:
Visit www.facthound.com
Type in this code: 9781515787839

Super-cool stuff!

Check out projects, games and lots more at
www.capstonekids.com

Index